W9-DDB-561

T·E·R·R·O·R·I·S·M

TERRORIST
GROUPS

By Michael Burgan

Content Adviser: Jarret Brachman, Ph.D., author of *Global Jihadism: Theory and Practice* and senior U.S. government counterterrorism consultant

Reading Adviser: Alexa L. Sandmann, Ed.D., Professor of Literacy, College and Graduate School of Education, Health, and Human Services, Kent State University

COMPASS POINT BOOKS
a capstone imprint

Compass Point Books
151 Good Counsel Drive
P.O. Box 669
Mankato, MN 56002-0669

Editor: Jennifer Fretland VanVoorst
Designer: Heidi Thompson
Media Researcher: Eric Gohl
Library Consultant: Kathleen Baxter
Production Specialist: Jane Klenk

Image Credits: AP Images/James Pringle, 11; AP Images/Nasser Ishtayeh, 16; AP
Images/Ricardo Mazalan, 25, cover; DVIC/NARA, 44; Getty Images Inc., 39; Getty
Images Inc./AFP, 27, 31, 35; Getty Images Inc./AFP/Gerry Penny, 9; Getty Images
Inc./AFP/Gonzalo Torres, 19; Getty Images Inc./AFP/Luis Acosta, 23; Getty Images
Inc./AFP/Romeo Gacad, 43; Getty Images Inc./AFP/Sena Vidanagama, 28; Getty
Images Inc./AFP/Yoshikazu Tsuno, 36; Getty Images Inc./Kaveh Kazemi, 7; Getty
Images Inc./Popperfoto/Rolls Press, 15; Getty Images Inc./Scott Peterson, 33; Getty
Images Inc./Time Life Pictures/David Rubinger, 40; Library of Congress, 5, 13;
Newscom/AFP Photo/Andreu Dalmau, 21.

This book was manufactured with paper containing
at least 10 percent post-consumer waste.

Library of Congress Cataloging-in-Publication Data
Burgan, Michael.
  Terrorist groups / by Michael Burgan.
     p. cm. — (Terrorism)
  Includes bibliographical references and index.
  ISBN 978-0-7565-4311-2 (library binding)
  1. Terrorists—Juvenile literature. 2. Terrorism—Juvenile
literature. I. Title. II. Series.
  HV6431.B865 2010
  363.325—dc22   2009034856

Visit Compass Point Books on the Internet at *www.compasspointbooks.com*
or e-mail your request to *custserv@compasspointbooks.com*

TABLE OF CONTENTS ///////////

WHAT IS ///////// TERRORISM?

On September 11, 2001, two jetliners crashed into the Twin Towers of New York City's World Trade Center. When the first plane hit, some people thought the crash was an accident. After another plane struck the second tower, President George W. Bush and other leaders assumed that terrorists had struck the United States.

Evidence soon proved that they were right. The 9/11 attacks were the latest in a series of terrorist acts against the United States. More than any previous bombings or killings, the 9/11 attacks made Americans aware of the dangers of terrorism.

The word *terrorism* was first used in the 1790s during the French Revolution. The idea of terrorism, however, is much older. Historians say the first organized terrorists appeared almost 2,000 years ago in Palestine—what is now Israel and part of Jordan.

Defining terrorism is not easy. People sometimes disagree about who a terrorist is and what a terrorist act is. Generally, however, terrorism is violence against people or property that is meant to create fear and disorder. It works because no one knows when other attacks will come or who will be targeted. Terrorists do not want to seize land or defeat an enemy on the battlefield. Instead they hope to create so much fear that others will accept their demands so the violence will end.

Terrorists create fear to promote a variety of goals. Some are seeking independence from a country or a change in the country's government. Some think their religious beliefs require them to attack people they see as enemies. But whatever their cause, terrorists think their acts of violence will help them reach a goal that their victims ignore, oppose, or don't understand.

The modern world is full of terrorist groups. They have appeared in many countries and had various goals. But all of them have shared the belief that creating fear through violence served their cause.

The terrorist attacks of September 11, 2001, made Americans keenly aware of the dangers of terrorism.

The Irish Republican Army: Decades of Terrorism

For more than 800 years, Irish Catholics hated British control of their homeland. The British were Protestants, and Catholics and Protestants in Europe had a history of conflict.

In 1916 a group called the Irish Republican Army fought a guerrilla war against British troops to win independence for Ireland. That conflict ended with the creation of the Irish Free State in 1922. (Today the country is called the Republic of Ireland.) Six counties in Northern Ireland remained under British control. That area, also called Ulster, had been settled by thousands of Protestants from England and Scotland who took over the Irish lands. Irish Catholics were a minority there.

Some members of the IRA did not accept this division of

Ireland and waged a two-year civil war, which ended with their defeat. But they continued to demand a united, independent country and used violence in an attempt to reach their goal.

A New IRA

By the late 1960s, a split had developed in the IRA. While some members wanted to promote a united socialist Ireland using peaceful political means, other members

Trainee members of the IRA received weapons instruction at a secret location outside Donegal, Ireland.

adopted terrorist methods. These militants said they hoped to "wash the British out of Ireland on a wave of blood." Thirty years of violence, known as the Troubles, began.

The minority Catholics in Northern Ireland, following the example of civil rights marchers in the United States, demanded an end to discrimination against them in jobs, politics, and living conditions. Their demands were met by violent crackdowns by the Protestant-dominated police force and illegal unionist paramilitary forces. The IRA responded with violence of its own.

At times the IRA tried to assassinate political leaders and other important people. In 1979 the group planted a bomb that killed Lord Mountbatten, a member of the British royal family. In another attack, the IRA tried to kill Margaret Thatcher, the head of the British government. The group

also killed police officers and British soldiers. Their attacks were met by increased violence by unionist paramilitaries determined to keep Ulster under British control.

The IRA also carried out random attacks on civilians across Great Britain. In 1978 a bomb killed 12 people in a restaurant in Belfast, Northern Ireland. In 1983 a car bomb went off outside Harrods, a famous London department store. The blast killed six people and wounded 90. In a few cases, the IRA carried out bombings against British targets in other countries. A 1988 attack in Germany wounded British soldiers stationed there.

A Political Solution?

The IRA killings continued through the 1990s. Several thousand people died as the IRA carried out attacks and battled British forces and paramilitary groups.

Very little remained of the Killyhelvin Hotel in Enniskillen, Northern Ireland, after a car bomb placed by the IRA exploded in July 1996.

Finally, in 1997, the head of Sinn Féin, a nationalist political party associated with the IRA, met with representatives from Great Britain. They and some Irish Protestants hoped to end the violence in Northern Ireland. Some IRA members rejected this effort and continued their terrorist attacks.

The worst bombing of the Troubles came in 1998, when an IRA splinter group killed 29 people in Omagh, Northern Ireland. Still the talks continued. Slowly the IRA gave up some of its weapons. Sinn Féin and the Irish Protestants began to share political power in Northern Ireland, though the British still controlled the six counties. In 2005 the IRA finally said it would no longer use violence to try to reach its goals. Yet some members were still ready to use terror to help unite Ulster with Ireland. In 2009 these violent members killed two British soldiers, stirring fears that the terrorism would go on.

IRGUN: CREATORS OF MODERN ISRAEL

The nation of Israel was born in 1948. The people who helped create it included members of a terrorist group called Irgun Zvai Leumi, which is Hebrew for National Military Organization. The group was commonly known as Irgun, and it had carried out violent acts for more than a decade.

Both ancient and modern events shaped the founding of Irgun. Several thousand years ago, the Jews created the first nation of Israel. They believed they were God's chosen people and God had given them the land. Over the centuries, foreign invasions ended Jewish control of Israel, and it became part of a region called Palestine. Most Jews spread out to live in other countries, and Arabs and other peoples settled in Palestine.

At the end of the 19th century, thousands of Jews began returning to Palestine. Some, called Zionists, hoped to create a new Jewish country there. In 1918 Great Britain took control of Palestine. The British said the Jews could create a homeland, but that the Arabs and other non-Jews there would keep their rights.

Many Arabs resisted the idea of a Jewish nation in Palestine, which was now their home. During the 1920s, violence broke out between Arabs and Jews.

Irgun Takes Action

During the conflicts, some Jews formed an underground army to battle the Arabs.

Armed members of Irgun took position on a Tel Aviv rooftop to be ready in case of Arab attack in December 1947.

Some members of this group wanted to take even more extreme action to create a Jewish state. Led by Vladimir Jabotinsky, these more militant Jews formed Irgun in 1937. When Arabs attacked Jews, Irgun responded by attacking Arabs. In May 1939, Irgun leaders began attacking British offices in Palestine. They hoped to force the British to create an independent Jewish state.

When World War II began a few months later, most Jews supported Britain and its allies in the fight against Germany. Some members of Irgun, however, formed a separate group known as the Stern Gang. They continued to attack the British in Palestine. In 1944 all of Irgun was once again attacking the British. The group blew up offices and police stations.

Terrorist to Peacemaker

In December 1943, Menachem Begin became the leader of Irgun. He thought violence was the only way to persuade the British to create the country of Israel. He said the Jews were fighting a revolution. The British, however, considered Begin and other members of Irgun terrorists. After Israel was created in 1948, Begin became the leader of one of its political parties. In 1977 he was elected prime minister. The following year, Begin helped end a state of war between Egypt and Israel. For his efforts, Begin was awarded the Nobel Peace Prize, which he shared with Egyptian leader Anwar Sadat.

Irgun carried out its deadliest terror attack after World War II. On July 22, 1946, Irgun blew up the King David Hotel in Jerusalem. The British army

British troops inspected the wreckage of the King David Hotel in Jerusalem shortly after it was bombed by Irgun in July 1946.

used part of the hotel as an office, but many civilians were also there when the blast occurred. Ninety-one people died, including some Jews, and many more were injured.

The next year, Irgun hanged two British soldiers after the British executed some of its members. The group also raided a prison to free dozens of its members. Irgun finally disbanded in 1948, after the United Nations created the new state of Israel. Most of its members joined the new Israeli army.

FATAH, ABU NIDAL, AND OTHERS: TERRORISM IN ///////////// PALESTINE

The creation of Israel in 1948 angered many Arabs who lived in what had been called Palestine. Hundreds of thousands of Palestinians fled to other Arab countries. During the 1950s, some of them formed groups to try to create a new Palestine by destroying Israel and taking its lands. A few of the groups turned to terror as one way to achieve their goal.

Fatah and Linked Groups

One of the first Palestinian terrorist groups was Fatah. Read backward, the letters of its name in Arabic stand for "Palestine Liberation Movement." Fatah formed in 1957 and was led by Yasir Arafat. He and his group joined the multiparty Palestine Liberation

Organization in 1968, and Arafat soon led that group, too.

In 1971 Fatah began attacking targets outside Israel. Its methods included hijackings and assassinations. Its worst terrorist act came during the 1972 Summer Olympics in Munich, Germany. By now Fatah was calling itself Black September.

Eight members went into the dormitory used by Israeli athletes. They killed two Israelis and took nine hostages. TV cameras showed the terrorists, wearing hoods and holding machine guns, as they demanded the release of several hundred Palestinian prisoners in Israel. The Palestinians eventually killed all of the hostages.

Mourners grieved over the caskets of Israeli athletes murdered by Black September during the 1972 Olympic Games.

The next year, Arafat, the PLO leader, decided that the PLO would not attack targets outside Israel. Abu Nidal, a member of the PLO, then created his own terror group to carry out international attacks. Named for him, the Abu Nidal Organization assassinated political leaders. It also used grenades and other weapons to attack public places. A 1982 attack on a Paris café killed six people and wounded 22. The group received support from Syria, Iraq, and Libya. It opposed Arafat's later efforts to peacefully create a Palestinian nation and allow Israel to exist. The Abu Nidal Organization operated through the 1990s, killing or wounding almost 900 people.

Other Palestinian Groups

In 1967 George Habbash formed the Popular Front for the Liberation of Palestine. Unlike Arafat and the PLO, Habbash wanted close ties with Arab nations. His group also opposed Arafat's later efforts to make peace with Israel. The

\\\\\\\ A member of the Popular Front for the Liberation of Palestine guarded a refugee camp in the Palestinian city of Nablus.

PFLP was most active during the 1970s and 1980s, when it sometimes used hot-air balloons and gliders to launch attacks on Israel. It also hijacked airliners, most famously one that was flown to Uganda in 1976. In a daring raid, Israeli commandos landed at the airport and freed the hostages on board.

A later Palestinian group, the Palestine Liberation Front, was formed in 1977. Its leaders also opposed any efforts to make peace with Israel. The PLF sometimes sneaked into Israel to take hostages, whom it would swap for Palestinians held in Israeli jails. The group also hijacked a cruise ship and killed a Jewish-American passenger who was in a wheelchair.

Most of the Palestinian groups that formed during the 1960s and 1970s still operate. Fatah is now a political organization based in Gaza, a region under Israeli control. Other PLO groups still carry out terrorist acts in Israel and the West Bank, another area Israel controls.

Pirates of the Air

Hundreds of years ago, pirates took over ships, seeking to steal riches. Since the 1930s, a new kind of pirate has sometimes taken control of airliners. These hijackers, as they're called, use guns or other weapons to force pilots to obey their orders. Terrorists began hijacking planes during the 1960s. In a 1969 hijacking, the Popular Front for the Liberation of Palestine took over three planes at once. The group landed them at airports in Lebanon and Egypt and blew them up. Al-Qaida hijacked four U.S. planes to carry out its 9/11 attacks. Since then, governments and airlines around the world have made it harder for passengers to take weapons aboard planes.

ETA: Terrorists
///////////////////// in Spain

For thousands of years, people known as Basques have lived in a region of the Pyrenees, mountains that separate France and Spain. The Basques speak a language unlike any other in Europe. Over the centuries, groups of foreign invaders have conquered their lands. Many Basques, though, have remained separate from these foreigners, even while under their control. Most of the Basque region has been part of Spain for centuries.

In 1959 some Basques formed ETA. The letters stand for the Basque words *Euzkadi ta Askatasuma,* which means "Basque Homeland and Freedom." By this time, Spain's leaders had outlawed the Basque language and arrested some Basque leaders who opposed the government. The founders of ETA wanted to unite the Basque lands in Spain and France and create an independent nation. They soon turned to terrorism to try to reach their goal.

Increasing Violence

ETA's first attack came in 1961. Some of its members used bombs to try to force a Spanish train off its tracks. They were unsuccessful. For several years after that, ETA did not carry out major attacks. Then in 1968, it assassinated a police chief. More assassinations and bombings followed. In 1973 ETA used a remote-controlled bomb to kill one of Spain's top political leaders. Most ETA targets had connections to the Spanish government or military, but some bombings also killed ordinary people.

A police officer inspected the wreckage of a car that exploded in Madrid in November 2001; the ETA bombing injured 95 people.

The number of killings rose through the 1970s. ETA bombing attacks in 1980 killed more than 100 people. At times the group also used grenades and rockets. To get money for their activities, group members robbed banks and kidnapped important people. ETA then collected a ransom to let the people go.

ETA members usually worked together in groups of three or four called cells. People in one cell rarely knew members of other cells. Some lived normal lives but secretly carried out terrorist activities. They often gathered information for ETA members who were in hiding. These members had to hide because the police knew they belonged to ETA. The underground members carried out the deadliest attacks.

Political Changes

In 1980 Spain gave its Basque region limited power to run its own affairs.

Some ETA members then formed a separate group to try to increase their control through politics. But more militant members kept fighting to achieve their goal of full independence. For a time, Josu Ternera led the terrorist attacks. He was arrested in 1989 and sent to prison. By this time, France and Spain were working together to arrest ETA members in both countries.

ETA shocked Spaniards in 1997 when the group killed one of its kidnap victims. Six million people filled the streets to protest the terrorist violence. The next year, ETA said it would stop its attacks. But in 1999 the Spanish government once again said it would not give the Basques independence. ETA soon returned to its violent ways.

A new leader for the group emerged. With Mikel Garikoitz

Demonstrators rallied in Barcelona to protest the ETA's killing of kidnapped politician Miguel Angel Blanco in July 1997.

Aspiazu Rubina in charge, ETA carried out more bombings. Some of its members were once again ready to talk to Spanish officials about ending the violence. Yet even after the arrest and imprisonment of Aspiazu Rubina in 2008, the more militant members continued to bomb various targets, killing and wounding ordinary people. The ETA said, "The resistance will continue as long as the rights of the Basque people are not recognized."

Many ETA leaders are behind bars, but no one expects the group to disappear or end its terrorist ways.

FARC: Terror and Drugs Combined

FARC is one of the oldest and largest terrorist groups in the world. Its name comes from the letters of its Spanish name, Fuerzas Armadas Revolucionarias de Colombia—Revolutionary Armed Forces of Colombia. FARC wants to create a Communist government in Colombia. Under that political system, a country has just one political party, the Communist Party, which controls the news media, the economy, and all other parts of society.

Roots of the Violence

During the 1950s, Colombia endured a long civil war known as La Violencia—the Violence. As many as 200,000 people were killed. In the countryside, groups of peasants sometimes united to protect themselves from attacks. Some of these groups later joined

Communists who wanted to use violence to seize power.

Manuel Marulanda was a peasant leader who embraced communism. In 1964 he created FARC to battle the government. Over the years, FARC grew, gaining as many as 18,000 members. The group controlled some parts of the Colombian countryside, but it also had supporters in the country's cities. FARC received aid from Cuba, which has a Communist government.

At times FARC acted as a rebel army, openly fighting Colombia's police and military. But during the 1970s, the group turned more to terrorist acts.

FARC operates a military academy where its members receive infantry training.

At times it kidnapped U.S. citizens visiting or living in Colombia and demanded ransoms for their release. FARC also bombed oil pipelines in Colombia and neighboring countries.

The Drug Trade

Ransoms from kidnappings helped FARC get more weapons and supplies. Most of its money, however, came from the illegal drug trade. Colombia is a major source of cocaine and heroin. FARC collected money from farmers who grew the crops used to make these drugs. They called the money a tax. Sometimes the terrorists made and sold the drugs themselves. FARC was soon making hundreds of millions of dollars every year through its drug business.

FARC grew so strong that in 1998, the government gave it control over an area of Colombia the size of Switzerland. The land was called a

Narco-terrorism

FARC is sometimes called a narco-terrorist group. *Narco* comes from the word *narcotic* and refers to certain strong drugs, such as opium and heroin. Narco-terrorists use the drug trade to finance their activities. They often work with powerful drug dealers who control large parts of the drug trade in a particular region. The terrorists protect growers and others in the trade from government arrest or attack. Narco-terrorism is also a major problem in Afghanistan. Poppies are the source of opium and heroin, and Afghan farmers grow most of the world's poppy supply. The terrorist group al-Qaida uses money from the poppy trade to pay for some of its attacks.

FARC members cleaned their rifles at their camp in the mountains near Miranda, Colombia.

"safe haven," where the military would not attack FARC. In return the group promised to begin peace talks. But it continued its bombings, kidnappings, and drug trade. In 2002 Colombia eliminated the safe haven and began a new military assault on the group. The U.S. government sent money to help in this effort, since it wanted to stop FARC from sending drugs to the United States.

By 2009 FARC was down to about 9,000 members and controlled a smaller part of Colombia—mostly its jungles. The group lost popular support because it sometimes killed peasants who refused to help the group. During that year, the Colombian government was able to free several hostages held by FARC. They included Ingrid Betancourt, a top Colombian politician. Although the group continued to plant bombs that sometimes killed ordinary people, Colombian leaders believed they were gaining in the battle against FARC.

TAMIL TIGERS:
/////////////// MODEL FOR
OTHER TERRORISTS

The tiny island nation of Sri Lanka lies in the Indian Ocean, just off the southeastern coast of India. The country is the home of one of the deadliest terrorist groups of all time, the Liberation Tigers of Tamil Eelam. More commonly called the Tamil Tigers, the group seeks to create regional self-rule for the Tamil people, an ethnic and religious minority. All together, the war they have fought against the Sri Lankan government has led to more than 70,000 deaths.

Rebels and Terrorists

A Tamil named Velupillai Prabhakaran formed the Tamil Tigers in 1976. It rose out of an earlier group with a similar name. Prabhakaran recruited other Tamils eager to fight for independence, including women and children. The group battles Sri Lankan military forces and carries out terrorist attacks against civilian leaders and ordinary people.

Of all the world's terrorist groups, only the Tamil Tigers have killed two world leaders. In 1991 they killed Rajiv Gandhi, the former head of India's government, who supported a peace plan they opposed. Two years later, the Tamil Tigers assassinated Ranasinghe Premadasa, the president of Sri Lanka. A bombing several years later wounded another Sri Lankan president.

The group's attacks have often left hundreds of casualties. A series of bombing attacks on buses in 1986 caused about 100 deaths. Less than a

Tamil women waved flags in support of the Tamil Tigers during a cultural festival in Sri Lanka.

year later, the Tigers set off a bomb at the main bus station in Colombo, the capital of Sri Lanka. The blast killed more than 100 people.

New Terror Tactics

Over the years, the Tamil Tigers have found new ways of causing terror. Experts say they used the first suicide bombers— people who blow themselves up in order

Female members of the Tamil Tigers guarded a road near Panchankerni, Sri Lanka.

to precisely hit their targets. The Tamil Tigers are also thought to have been the first terrorist group with female suicide bombers. Many terrorists in the Middle East and Asia have copied these methods.

The Tamil Tigers have trained swimmers to carry out suicide attacks on Sri Lankan naval ships. Tamil fighters wear poison pills around their necks. If caught they take the poison rather than face questioning or going to jail.

In 2008 and 2009, Sri Lanka's military increased its efforts to destroy the Tamil Tigers. Both the government and the terrorist group drew international criticism for endangering thousands of ordinary people while fighting. In May 2009, the military announced that it had killed the Tamil Tigers' leader and defeated the rebels.

Young Tigers

The Tamil Tigers sometimes force boys as young as 14 to join the group. Other teens join willingly, especially if their parents belong. The Tigers train the youths to shoot guns, plant bombs, and kill with machetes. The young Tigers receive the same poison pills the adults do, though some choose not to use them when they are caught. One teen who refused to kill himself told a reporter in 2009, "I wanted a future." He ended up at a special camp run by the United Nations for young Tamils who once fought for the Tigers. The U.N. and the Sri Lankan government want to train the former terrorists so they will have jobs and will not need to go back to the Tigers to earn money to support their families.

HEZBOLLAH:
////////// ENEMIES OF ISRAEL

Starting in the early 1970s, Israel faced attacks from Palestinian terrorists based in Lebanon. Hoping to end most of the attacks, the Israelis invaded that neighboring country. But the war in Lebanon led to the rise of a new terrorist group, Hezbollah.

Hezbollah means Party of God. Its founders were deeply religious, unlike the leaders of the Palestine Liberation Organization and other early Arab terrorist groups. Hezbollah's members follow Shi'ism, one branch of Islam. From its founding, the group received help from Iran, the only Shi'ite nation in the Middle East. Iran's leaders wanted to strengthen Shi'ism in the region and to force Israel to give back land it had won in two earlier wars. Hezbollah shared these goals, and some of its leaders said Israel had no right to exist at all. The group carried out attacks against Israel and its supporters, mainly the United States.

Bombings and Kidnappings

Terrorists calling themselves Islamic Jihad set off a car bomb at the U.S. Embassy in Beirut, Lebanon, in April 1983. The blast killed 49 people.

Islamic Jihad soon became a part of Hezbollah, and a few months later it carried out an even deadlier attack. This time suicide bombers killed more than 300 international troops who had been trying to keep peace in Lebanon. The dead included 241 U.S. troops. The suicide bombers gladly gave their

Newly sworn in Hezbollah fighters salute during a ceremony in the Lebanese town of Qana in 2009.

lives, since Shi'ite leaders had told them they were doing the work of Allah, the Muslim name for God. The bombers expected to be rewarded for their actions when they reached heaven.

Over the next several years, Hezbollah members kidnapped or assassinated dozens of Americans and Europeans in Lebanon. It also trained Palestinian terrorists who launched attacks against Israel. Although the rest of the world saw Hezbollah members as terrorists, Lebanese Shi'ites supported the group. In 1992 voters elected eight members of Hezbollah to serve in the country's government.

Hezbollah did function partly as a political party. It ran its own television and radio stations. It also set up schools and other public services in southern Lebanon. But Hezbollah continued to carry out terrorist attacks, especially against Jews. A 1994 bomb blast at a Jewish community center in Buenos Aires, Argentina, killed 94 people. Hezbollah fired rockets into Israel in 2006 and kidnapped two Israeli soldiers. In response, Israel attacked Hezbollah positions in southern Lebanon.

Uncertain Future

Since 1992 Hassan Nasrallah has led Hezbollah. He has helped the group gain an even larger role in Lebanon's politics. At times he has spoken out against terrorism committed by other groups. Yet he says Palestinians have a right to carry out suicide bombings in Israel. In recent years Hezbollah has lost some support in Lebanon, because people blamed the group for causing Israel to attack in 2006. Israel remains determined to defend itself against attacks carried out by Hezbollah.

Citizens of Barachit, Lebanon, carried the casket of a citizen killed in the 2006 Israeli-Hezbollah conflict.

AUM SHINRIKYO: PLANNING THE END OF ///////////// THE WORLD

During the early 1990s, a small Japanese religious group turned to terrorism to carry out its founder's aims. Shoko Asahara had started Aum Shinrikyo—Japanese for Supreme Truth—in 1987. Asahara claimed he had special knowledge about the future. He predicted that a new world war would soon kill most of the world's people. Only he and his followers would survive, he said. By turning to violence, Asahara wanted to help make the war and destruction come true.

Building a Terrorist Cult

Aum Shinrikyo was a cult, a small religious group headed by a single powerful, extremist leader. Asahara claimed to be the world's first "enlightened one" since the Buddha, the founder of Buddhism who lived in India more than 2,500 years ago. Asahara sought bright, wealthy Japanese college students to join his cult. Asahara used their knowledge to create successful businesses.

Aum Shinrikyo made money running computer stores and restaurants. Asahara then took the profits and built a science lab. He hired scientists to create deadly

Aum Shinrikyo leader Shoko Asahara practiced acupuncture and Chinese medicine before forming his religious cult.

germs and chemicals. Instead of using guns and bombs, Aum Shinrikyo spread the germs and chemicals to try to kill and injure people.

Aum Shinrikyo members made their first attack in 1990. They spread a mist around government buildings in downtown Tokyo, Japan's capital. The mist contained botulin, a deadly germ. The attack failed, however. No one inhaled the mist, or if they did, it was not strong enough to harm them. A few years later, the group tried to spread anthrax, another deadly germ. Once again it was unsuccessful.

||||||

Members of Aum Shinrikyo were often seen wearing headgear they were told would transmit their leader's brainwaves to them.

Deadly Gas Attack

Asahara's scientists then produced a deadly chemical called sarin, which causes muscles and body organs to work faster than normal. Aum Shinrikyo carried out a sarin attack in Matsumoto, Japan, in June 1994, killing seven people. The next year, group members released sarin in several subway cars in Tokyo. This time 12 people died, and as many as 6,000 went to hospitals to be treated. The attack shocked the world. It was the worst terrorist attack ever in Japan.

Japanese police soon tracked down Asahara and other members of Aum Shinrikyo. Asahara was sentenced to die for his role in the sarin attacks. Aum Shinrikyo changed its name to Aleph and still exists, though it has not carried out other terrorist attacks.

Weapons of Mass Destruction

When used to kill a large number of people, germs and chemicals are called weapons of mass destruction. A small amount of these weapons can harm many people at one time. They can be spread through the air, such as by being released from exploding bombs or rockets. They can also be put into food and water supplies. Another type of WMD is nuclear weapons. Most WMDs are controlled by governments, but Aum Shinrikyo's activities showed that terrorist groups could also acquire and use some WMDs.

HAMAS: SEEKING AN ISLAMIC PALESTINE

The struggle over land in the Middle East has led to some of the worst terrorism in history. By the end of the 20th century, Hamas had emerged as one of the most dangerous groups in the region. The letters in *Hamas* stand for Arabic words that mean Islamic Resistance Movement. Hamas is also Arabic for *courage*.

Like the PLO, Hamas is made up of Palestinians seeking a homeland in what is now Israel. Like Hezbollah, Hamas wants that Palestinian state to strictly follow the Islamic religion. Hamas' members, however, are Sunni, members of the largest branch of Islam, while Hezbollah is a Shi'ite Muslim group. And unlike the PLO, Hamas denies that Jews have a right to claim any land for themselves in what was once Palestine.

Roots in Egypt

The roots of Hamas are in a group called the Muslim Brotherhood. It formed in Egypt in 1928, seeking to end secular rule in Arab nations. The group thought those nations should follow the laws set down in the Qur'an, the Islamic holy book.

Separate branches of the Muslim Brotherhood sprang up across the Middle East.

In 1967 during a six-day war, Israel won control of Gaza and the West Bank, lands that were once controlled by Arab nations. Muslim Brotherhood member Ahmed Yassin then came

Masked members of Hamas dressed as suicide bombers marched in support of Izzedine al-Masri, who blew himself up in a 2001 attack on Jerusalem.

Thousands of Arabs surged out of the Nusseirat refugee camp to protest Israeli rule during the Palestinian uprising of 1987.

to Gaza to set up a political and educational organization. Palestinians in Gaza and the West Bank began to rebel against Israeli rule in 1987. Their uprising and violent acts against Israel were called the *intifada*—meaning rebellion. Yassin founded

Hamas that year to carry out terrorist attacks against Israeli targets.

The Violence Begins

Hamas called for a *jihad*, a holy war, against Israel. It carried out its first terrorist acts in 1989, shooting dozens of Israelis. Five years later, it began car bombings in Israel. The first one killed eight people. Hamas also used suicide bombers, recruiting young, religious men to carry out these attacks. A suicide bomber blew up an Israeli bus, killing 22 people, in 1994. In later attacks, suicide bombers set off deadly explosions in restaurants, hotels, and other public buildings. Hamas gave the families of the dead bombers money and assured them their relatives had given their lives for a holy struggle.

Over the years, the car bombs and suicide attacks continued. Hamas also began launching rockets into Israel. The attacks often targeted ordinary people, not soldiers. To pay for its actions, Hamas relied on money sent from Palestinians living abroad. Other Arabs also donated money, and Iran sent the group millions of dollars every year. Along with funding terrorism, Hamas used some of its money to run schools and provide health care in Gaza. This helped the group build popular support.

A Changing Role

Israel let the Palestinians of Gaza run some of their local affairs. Members of Hamas won elections in 2006 that gave them control of the region's lawmaking body. The victory led Israel to shut off the borders into Gaza. It wanted to prevent Hamas from receiving new weapons. Twice between 2006 and 2009 Israel bombed Gaza, seeking to weaken Hamas. But the group still refused to recognize that Israel has a right to exist, and it continued to use terror to reach its goals. No one knows when peace will come to Gaza and the rest of the region.

AL-QAIDA: TERROR FUELED BY RELIGION

Troops from the Soviet Union invaded Afghanistan on December 25, 1979. Their goal was to create an Afghan government that would be friendly to the Soviet Union. For almost 10 years, the Afghans battled the Soviet troops. Finally they forced the Soviets to leave the country. Helping the Afghans were Arab fighters from foreign countries. These fighters later became the core of al-Qaida, whose name is Arabic for the Base.

One of the Arab leaders in Afghanistan was Abdullah Azzam. He was a devout scholar of Islam and believed that the Afghans and Arabs were fighting a jihad against the Soviet Union. After the Soviet troops left Afghanistan, Azzam and others, including Osama bin Laden, founded al-Qaida to continue the war. This time Azzam said devout

Muslims should fight the Jewish nation of Israel and powerful, largely Christian nations, such as the United States. Azzam wanted to create a new Islamic empire. Hundreds of years ago, Islamic governments controlled the Middle East, Central Asia, North Africa, and parts of southern Europe. Azzam believed

Muslims should rule those lands again. After Azzam was assassinated in 1989, Osama bin Laden emerged as the leader of al-Qaida.

U.S. and European troops arrived in Saudi Arabia in 1991. They were there to turn back an invasion of neighboring Kuwait by Iraq. Saudi Arabia was the

Al-Qaida militants in the Philippines guarded a mosque where their leaders were negotiating the release of hostages.

birthplace of Islam. Two of the religion's holiest cities are there. Bin Laden became angry that infidel—non-Muslim—troops were now based in Saudi Arabia. He also accused the United States and its allies of carrying out or supporting the mass killing of Muslims in many countries.

The Attacks Begin

Bin Laden set up camps in Sudan and later Afghanistan to train radical Muslims to fight against soldiers from Israel and mostly Christian nations. The terrorists learned how to read maps, use bombs, fire weapons, and fight in hand-to-hand combat. Cells of trained terrorists then settled in several countries. They waited to receive instructions from al-Qaida to carry out terrorist attacks. U.S. military officials considered al-Qaida the greatest terrorist threat to the country. Thanks to bin Laden, its members were well-armed and well-trained, and they had plenty of money.

A poster of al-Qaida leader Osama bin Laden was used to glorify the group's cause and recruit new members.

Al-Qaida's first attacks came in 1998, as members set off bombs at U.S. embassies in Tanzania and Kenya. The explosions killed more than 200 people. The deadliest al-Qaida attacks came on September 11, 2001. Four teams of terrorists hijacked U.S. airliners, crashing two of the aircraft into the World Trade Center in New York City. Another struck the Pentagon, the headquarters of the U.S. military. The fourth crashed into a Pennsylvania field. All together, almost 3,000 people died in the attacks.

President George W. Bush said the United States was at war with al-Qaida and any countries that helped it. In October U.S. and British soldiers arrived in Afghanistan. They hunted for bin Laden, but he managed to escape into the mountains that separate Afghanistan and Pakistan.

In the years after 2001, the United States and its allies killed or captured many al-Qaida leaders. But some group members were able to return to Afghanistan. Al-Qaida also carried out attacks in other parts of the world. U.S. President Barack Obama said his top goal was to stop al-Qaida. The small number of Muslims who share al-Qaida's views are determined to keep fighting.

Continuing Threat

No one knows when or where the next terrorist attack will occur. Although governments around the world are working to stop terrorists before they strike, these groups probably will continue to have occasional successes. Terrorist groups have been around for a long time, and the threat they pose is unlikely to disappear anytime soon.

GLOSSARY

allies—friends and supporters of a person or country, especially during wartime

assassinate—to muder someone who is well-known or important, often for political reasons

casualties—people killed or wounded in an attack

cells—subgroups of a larger organization

civilians—citizens not in the military

embassy—residence and office of a country's officials in a foreign country

enlightened—having an unusual amount of knowledge about something

hijacking—forcefully taking control of a vehicle, usually a plane

hostages—people held against their will

infidel—unbeliever with respect to a particular religion

Islam—religion founded on the Arabian Peninsula in the seventh century by the prophet Muhammad; believers say he was the last human to speak for God, and that his teachings must be followed

militant—person ready to use violence to reach a goal

nationalists—people who want their nation to be independent from foreign rule or influence

paramilitary forces—illegally armed groups with a political purpose

ransom—money paid to release people who are held against their will

secular—nonreligious or separate from religious beliefs

Soviet Union—communist nation formed in 1922 when Russia combined with 14 other republics in eastern Europe and central Asia; it broke apart in 1991

underground—in hiding; hidden or secret

ADDITIONAL RESOURCES

Further Reading

Espejo, Roman, ed. *What Motivates Suicide Bombers?* Detroit: Greenhaven Press, 2009.

Gupta, Dipak K. *Who Are the Terrorists?* New York: Chelsea House, 2006.

Katz, Samuel M. *At Any Cost: National Liberation Terrorism.* Minneapolis: Lerner Publications, 2004.

Landau, Elaine. *Suicide Bombers: Foot Soldiers of the Terrorist Movement.* Minneapolis: Twenty-First Century Books, 2007.

Langley, Andrew. *September 11: Attack on America.* Minneapolis: Compass Point Books, 2006.

Levin, Jack. *Domestic Terrorism.* New York: Chelsea House, 2006.

Internet Sites

FactHound offers a safe, fun way to find Internet sites related to this book. All of the sites on FactHound have been researched by our staff.

Here's all you do:
Visit *www.facthound.com*
FactHound will fetch the best sites for you!

Look for other books in this series:

Combating Terrorism
The History of Terrorism
What Makes a Terrorist?

Select Bibliography

Anderson, Sean K., and Stephen Sloan. *Historical Dictionary of Terrorism.* Lanham, Md.: Scarecrow Press, 2009.

Avi-Yonah, Michael, ed. *A History of Israel and the Holy Land.* New York: Continuum Publishing Group, 2001.

Chaliand, Gérard, and Arnaud Blin. *The History of Terrorism: From Antiquity to Al Qaeda.* Berkeley: University of California Press, 2007.

Combs, Cindy C., and Martin Slann. *Encyclopedia of Terrorism.* New York: Facts on File, 2002.

Laqueur, Walter. *A History of Terrorism.* New Brunswick, N.J.: Transaction Publishers, 2001.

Rotella, Sebastian. "Trial Shows Al-Qaeda Is Still Gunning for West—but Failing." *Los Angeles Times*, 11 Sept. 2008. 24 Sept. 2009. http://articles.latimes.com/2008/sep/11/world/fg-qaeda11

Schweimler, Daniel. "Analysis: Basque Pride." BBC News, 6 Dec. 1999. 24 Sept. 2009. http://news.bbc.co.uk/2/hi/europe/548545.stm

Westhead, Rick: "Born to Be a Tamil Tiger: A Child Soldier's Tale." *The Toronto Star*, 17 Feb. 2009. 24 Sept. 2009. www.thestar.com/article/588507

Index

About the Author

Michael Burgan is a freelance writer of books for children and adults. A history graduate of the University of Connecticut, he has written more than 200 fiction and nonfiction children's books. For adult audiences, he has written news articles, essays, and plays. Michael Burgan is a recipient of an Educational Press Association of America award.